CURIOUS questions and answers about...

Astronauts

Words by Sue Becklake
Illustrations by Pauline Reeves

WINDMILL BOOKS™

Published in 2022 by Windmill Books,
an Imprint of Rosen Publishing
29 East 21st Street, New York, NY 10010

Cataloging-in-Publication Data

Names: Becklake, Sue, author. | Reeves, Pauline, illustrator.
Title: Astronauts / written by Sue Becklake, illustrated by Pauline Reeves.
Description: New York : Windmill Books, 2022. | Series: Curious questions and answers about...
Identifiers: ISBN 9781499487664 (pbk.) | ISBN 9781499487688 (library bound) | ISBN 9781499487671 (6 pack) | ISBN 9781499487695 (ebook)
Subjects: LCSH: Astronauts--Juvenile literature. | Outer space--Exploration--Juvenile literature.
Classification: LCC TL793.B388 2022 | DDC 629.45 --dc23

Manufactured in the United States of America

CPSIA Compliance Information: Batch BS22WM: For Further Information contact Rosen Publishing, New York, New York at 1-800-237-9932

CURIOUS questions and answers about...

Astronauts

Words by Sue Becklake

Illustrations by Pauline Reeves

What is an astronaut?

An astronaut is a specially trained person who leaves Earth to travel into space. All around Earth, space stretches out between the distant planets and stars.

Why do astronauts go into space?

To explore different places, such as the moon, and to find out what it is like to live in space.

How long do they spend in space?

Astronauts usually stay on the International Space Station (ISS) for six months, but four astronauts have spent over a year in space.

Most astronauts go to the ISS, which is 643 miles above Earth. The farthest astronauts have been is to the moon— 238,850 miles away.
Rocket launched from Earth
Earth

How do astronauts get into space?

① Launching into space

A huge, powerful rocket launches the Soyuz spacecraft, with three astronauts inside, into space.

② Rocket separation

When the rocket is 30 miles up, its boosters separate. By the time it is 125 miles into space, the Soyuz spacecraft has separated from the rocket.

③ Circling Earth

The astronauts sit snugly in seats inside the spacecraft as it orbits Earth.

4 Docking

The spacecraft catches up with the ISS and locks on to it. The astronauts can then climb on board to meet the ISS crew.

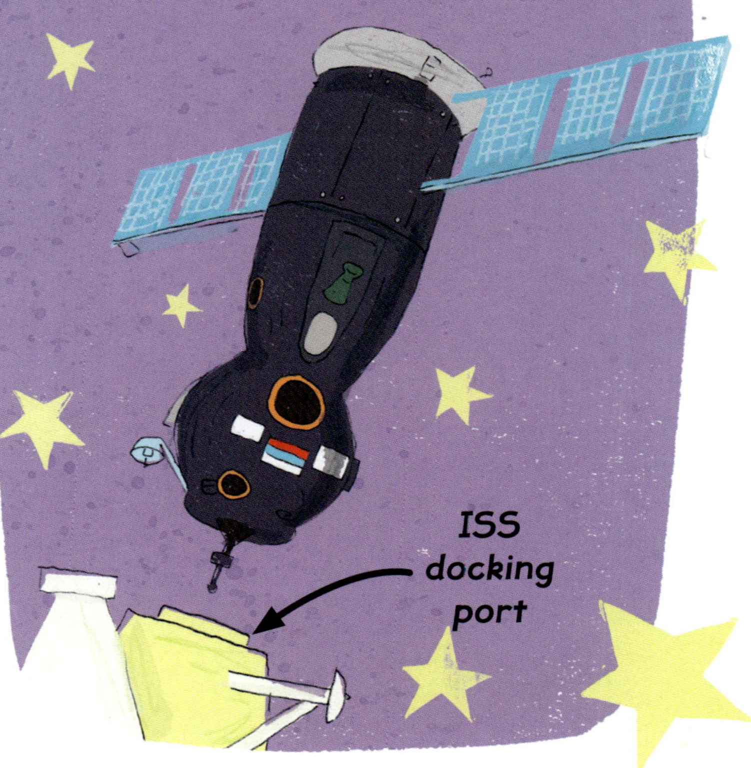

5 Heading home

When the Soyuz spacecraft re-enters the air around Earth, it is going extremely fast. The outside rubs against the air and gets incredibly hot, but the astronauts are safe inside. It's a bumpy ride, though!

6 Safe landing

Astronauts feel nothing more than a bump when they land on the ground. They are helped onto recliners because their legs are weak after months of living in space.

Can anyone be an astronaut?

Any adult person who is fit and healthy can travel in space. Astronauts who go to the ISS have months of training, but in the future ordinary people may be able to go to space.

How do astronauts get used to floating in space?

In a big airplane flying in loops, trainee astronauts float for a short time as though they were weightless.

How do trainees practice space walks?

Wearing spacesuits underwater, they float in a huge tank. They can practice everything they will do when they go on space walks.

What special skills do they need?

Astronauts have to learn how everything on the space station works and how to fix it if something goes wrong. They also practice doing the experiments planned for their space trip.

Aspiring astronauts need to be very healthy because there are no hospitals in space. They also need to know about science or engineering.

Did you know?

Astronauts built the **ISS**, joining the parts together in space.

Russian cosmonaut Yuri Gagarin was the **first person** to fly into space on April 10, 1961.

Between 1981 and 2011, American **space shuttles** carried astronauts into space. The shuttles flew many times, taking off like a rocket and landing back on a runway like a plane.

Spacewalking astronauts use a **tether** to fix themselves to the ISS so they can't float off.

You can sometimes see the ISS moving slowly across the sky like a **bright star** just after sunset.

Astronauts add **liquid** salt and pepper to their food. Grains or powder would float around and get into vital equipment.

The first person to walk on the **moon**, in July 1969, was Neil Armstrong.

Many astronauts get **space sick**, like motion sickness, but it soon wears off.

The first female astronaut, and the only **woman** to fly solo in space, was Valentina Tereshkova in 1963.

Peggy Whitson was the first **female commander** of the ISS, in 2007 and 2016.

There have been **seven** astronaut tourists who have paid millions of dollars to fly to the ISS.

What do astronauts wear?

Inside a space station, they wear ordinary clothes, but outside astronauts need a spacesuit to keep them alive. Spacesuits are very expensive—each costs about $12 million.

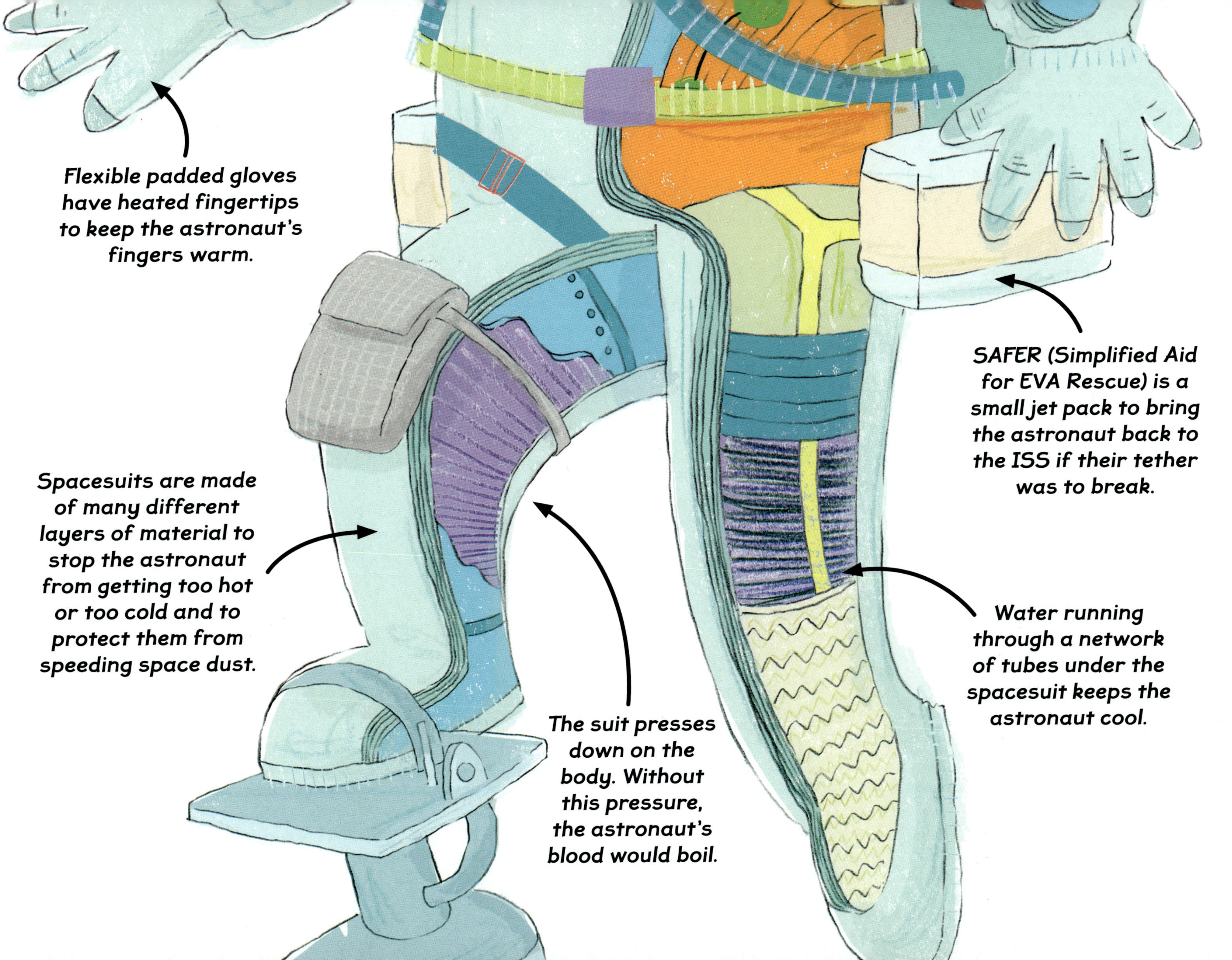
Flexible padded gloves have heated fingertips to keep the astronaut's fingers warm.
Spacesuits are made of many different layers of material to stop the astronaut from getting too hot or too cold and to protect them from speeding space dust.
The suit presses down on the body. Without this pressure, the astronaut's blood would boil.
SAFER (Simplified Aid for EVA Rescue) is a small jet pack to bring the astronaut back to the ISS if their tether was to break.
Water running through a network of tubes under the spacesuit keeps the astronaut cool.

Where do astronauts live?

The International Space Station, which is circling Earth, is home to astronauts exploring space. It is made of sections called modules where astronauts can eat, sleep, and work.

Does everything float in a space station?

Yes! On Earth, gravity pulls everything down to the ground, but in a space station, the astronauts and everything else, like food, water, and tools, float around if they are not fixed down. We say they are weightless.

Docking area

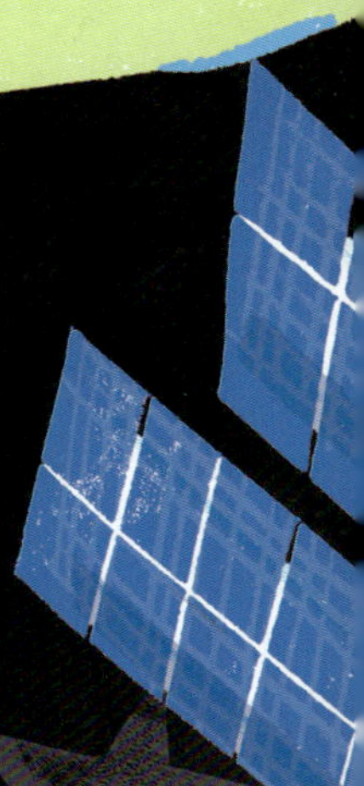

International Space Station

How do astronauts get food and water?

Everything they need is delivered from Earth in a Soyuz spacecraft or a robot ferry.

I wear earplugs and an eye mask to keep out the noise and light so I can sleep.

How many?

The number of astronauts who have flown in space is over

500.

3

gallons of water is all an astronaut uses each day (compared to 34 gallons for an average person on Earth).

12

astronauts have walked on the moon so far.

2912° Fahrenheit

The approximate temperature a spacecraft heats up to when it plunges back into the air around Earth.

62

The height in miles above Earth where space officially begins.

17,400

The speed in miles per hour a spacecraft must reach to stay in space and not fall back to Earth.

The ISS has a supply of about **632** gallons of water but over 90 percent of it, including toilet water and sweat, is recycled!

Astronauts from **18** different countries have lived on the ISS.

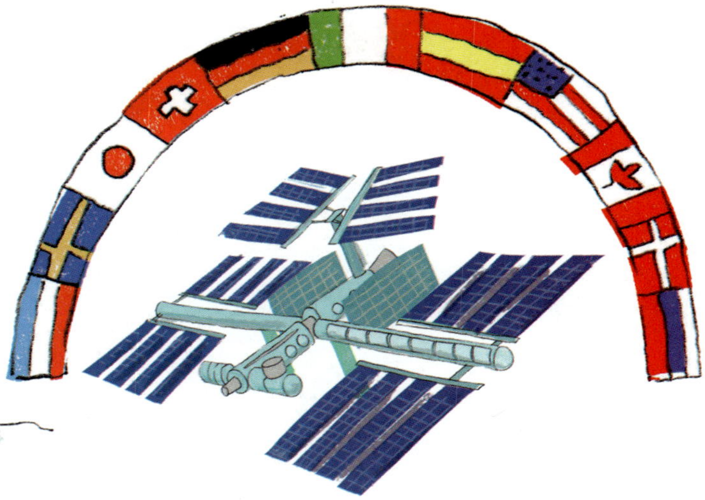

The oldest astronaut so far is John Glenn. He went into space at the age of **77**.

3 The number of days it took the Apollo astronauts to get to the moon.

A spacesuit backpack provides an astronaut with about **8.5** hours of oxygen and water and enough nitrogen gas for the SAFER jet thrusters to power back to the ISS.

What do astronauts eat?

They eat the same things as you and choose their favorite foods before they go. The food is cooked on Earth and then sent to the space station in ready-to-eat portions.

We've just had a delivery of fresh fruit from Earth. We'll have to eat it quickly because we don't have a fridge to keep it fresh.
Orange
Apple
Beef and mashed potatoes
We don't eat crumbly foods like bread because the crumbs float around and get stuck in equipment.
Chicken and rice
Pancake

Why do astronauts exercise in space?

Exercise helps to keep the astronauts strong and healthy. Their bodies change in space without gravity to pull them down to the ground. They get taller, and their bones and muscles get weaker.

Weightlifting in space doesn't build up muscle because the weights feel as light as a feather! Instead we pull or push against strong springs.

British astronaut Tim Peake ran 26.2 miles, the same distance as the London marathon, on a treadmill in the ISS in April 2016.

Couldn't they just run around the ISS?

No, astronauts need straps to hold them down to each piece of equipment and provide resistance for their muscles.

Do they come home looking different?

Astronauts can get up to two inches taller because the bones in their backs stretch apart without gravity pulling them together. Weightlessness can also make their faces look puffy.

What jobs are done in space?

Astronauts are very busy. They look after the ISS, keep it clean and tidy, and repair anything that goes wrong. They also do lots of experiments.

Who cleans the ISS?

Everyone helps to clean once a week. Astronauts use a vacuum cleaner to remove dust. They also check that everything is working well and fix it if not.

What experiments do astronauts do?

They try to find out how things such as crystals and plants grow differently in space.

What is an EVA?

Extravehicular activity (EVA) is the name for a spacewalk. This is when astronauts put on spacesuits to work outside the space station, installing new equipment or doing repairs.

Do astronauts have robot helpers?

Yes! Canadarm2 is a robot arm on the outside of the ISS. Astronauts operate it from inside, and it can help to move or install bulky parts.

Why do astronauts take living things into space?

They study how things behave differently in space. They grow seeds, and they watch insects and small animals to study how quickly they get used to weightlessness.

Would you rather?

Eeuww, stinky smells! Would you rather live in the **sealed** ISS or on Earth where you can just **open** a window?

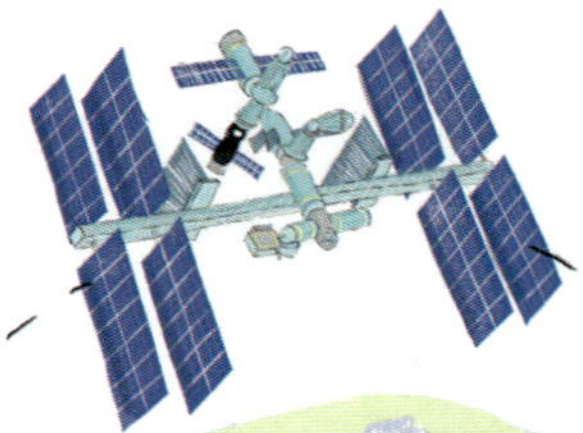

Would you rather **live** in a space station circling Earth or **travel** for six months to visit Mars?

Time for pooping practice! Would you prefer a **comfy toilet** at home or aiming at a teeny hole on a **space toilet**?

If you were working in space, would you prefer to **suit up** for a spacewalk outside or stay inside in **pajamas** to operate a robot arm?

Would you rather watch spiders **spin webs** or ants **build tunnels** in weightlessness?

Would you prefer to float inside a **space station** or float around a **swimming pool** on Earth?

Would you rather play **golf** on the moon (like astronaut Alan Shepard in 1971) or **table tennis** on the ISS?

Would you prefer to look down at **Earth** from the ISS or stare at the **moon** from Earth through a telescope?

Can astronauts take a bath?

Astronauts don't bathe in space, because water would not run out of a faucet or stay in a bath. Water turns into balls of liquid that float around.

How about having a shower instead?

The US Skylab space station in 1973 did have a shower. It was sealed shut to keep all the water inside and the astronauts had to vacuum up the water before they could get out.

How do they brush their teeth?

Do astronauts do laundry?

Astronauts save water by not washing their clothes. They throw away their underwear and socks, but keep wearing the same outer clothes for about six weeks!

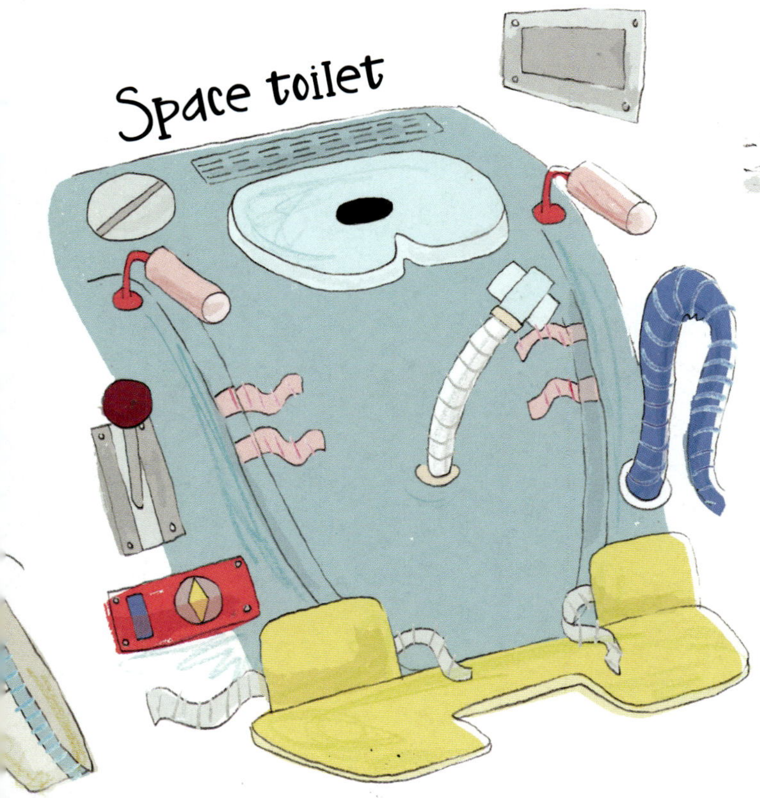

Where does their poo go?

Space toilets do not use water for flushing. Flowing air sucks the waste away into bags to be recycled or taken back to Earth. Astronauts have to fix themselves down so they stay on the toilet.

Will people ever visit Mars?

Yes, there are plans to send people to Mars. The journey will take six months each way. They will have to take everything they need to stay alive—food, water, and air to breathe.

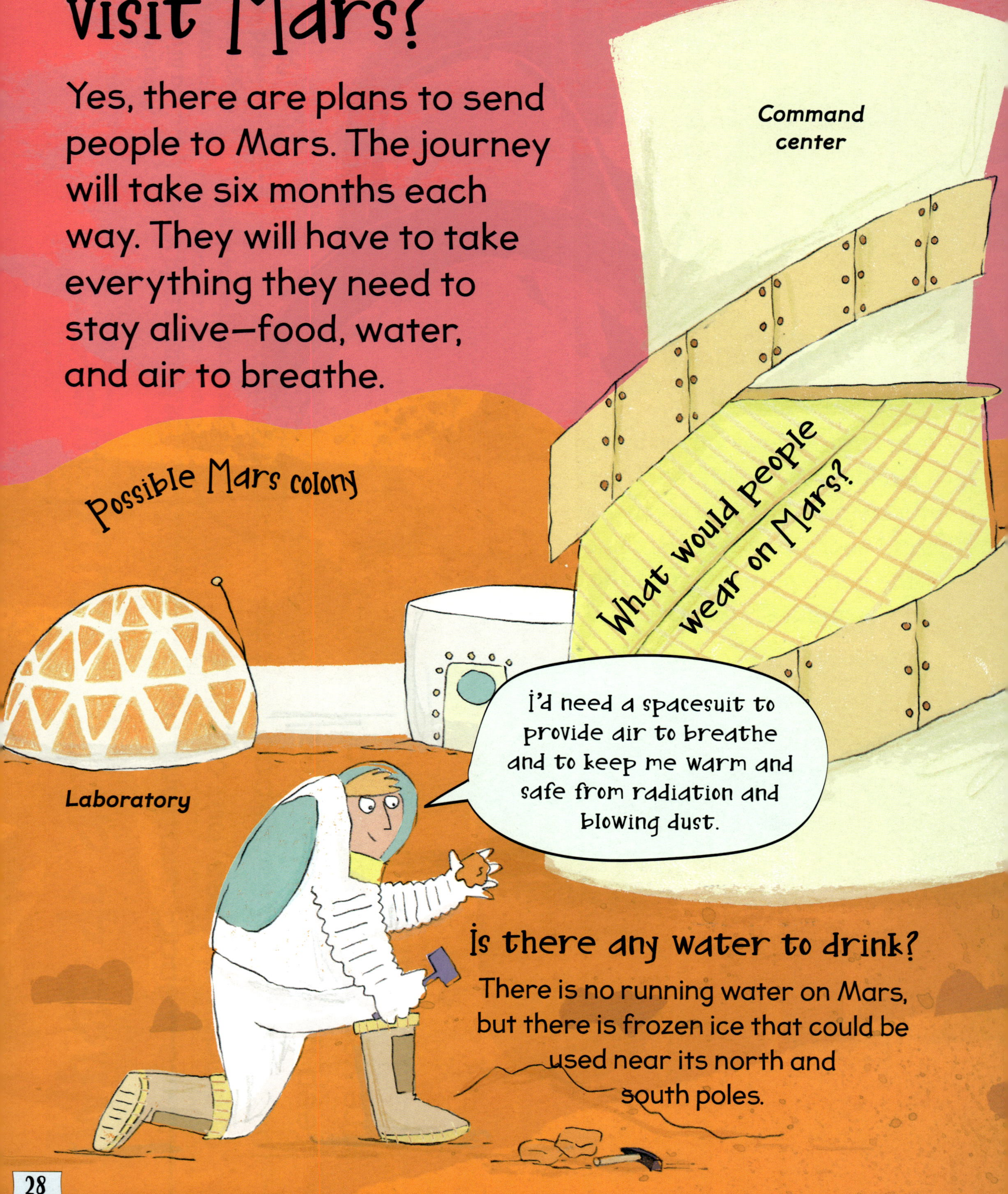

Is there any water to drink?

There is no running water on Mars, but there is frozen ice that could be used near its north and south poles.

Could people sunbathe on Mars?

It would be far too cold! Mars is farther from the sun than Earth. It's also dry and windy, and there are often huge dust storms.

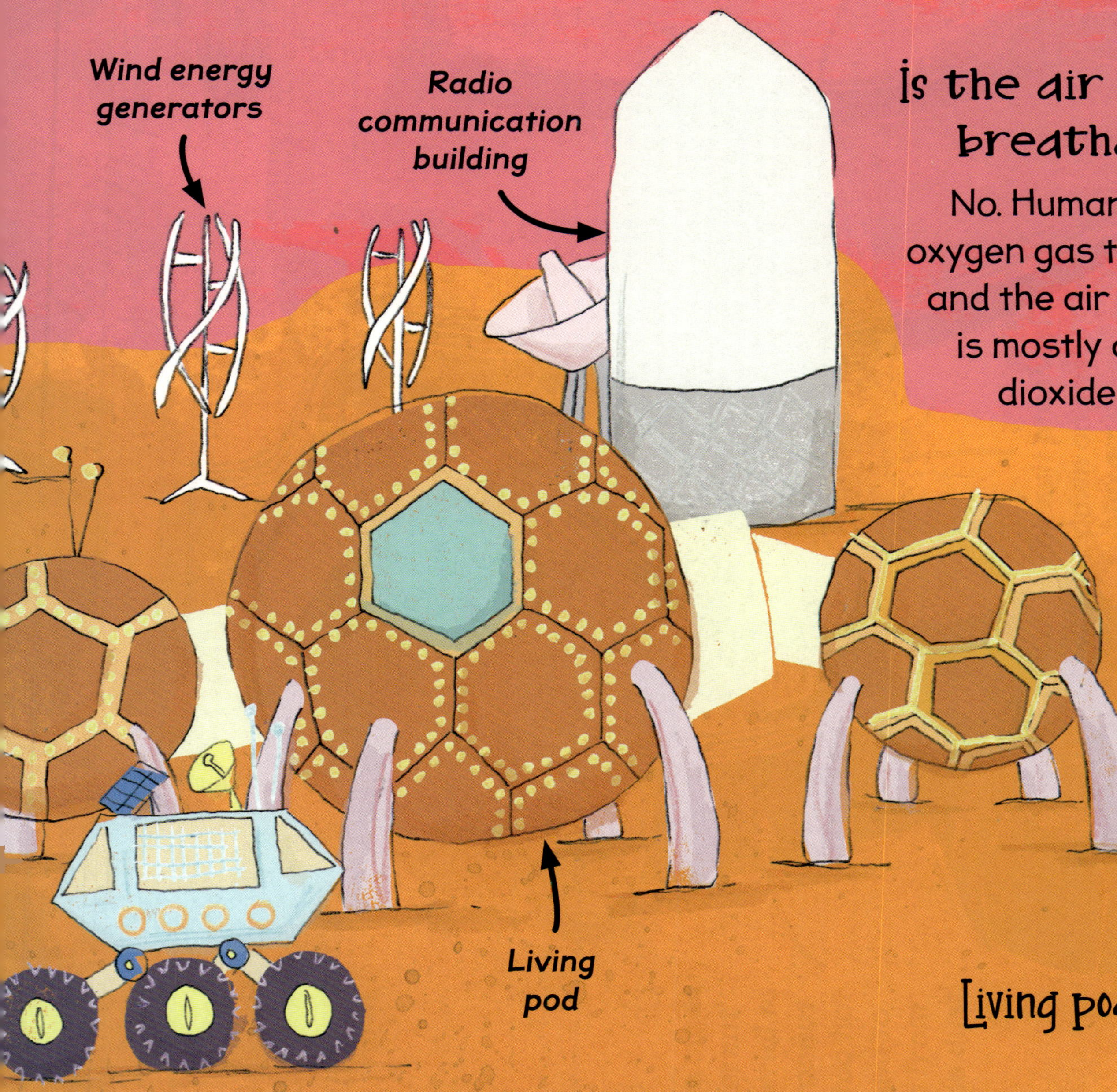

Is the air on Mars breathable?

No. Humans need oxygen gas to breathe and the air on Mars is mostly carbon dioxide gas.

Where could they live?

If astronauts built homes on Mars, they would need thick walls to protect against dangerous radiation. They might even build homes underground.

A compendium of questions

How often do astronauts see a sunrise?

They see the sun rise and set 16 times every day from the ISS as it circles Earth.

How big is the ISS?

The living space inside is bigger than a six-bedroom house. The whole station stretches out to about the size of a sports field.

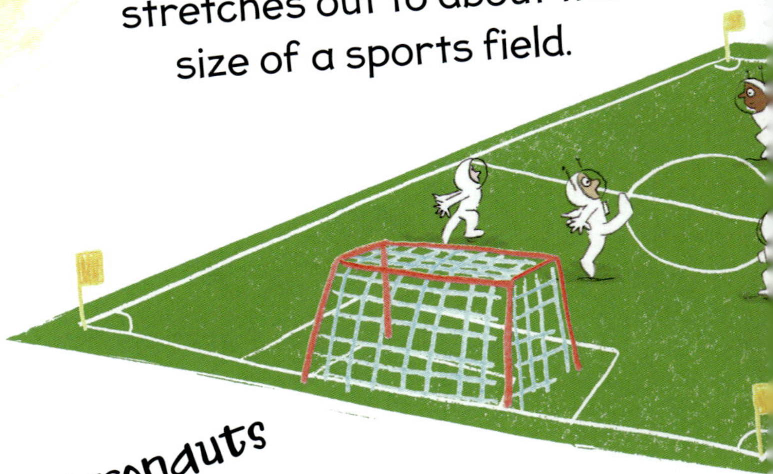

How many astronauts live on the ISS?

Usually six, but there are nine when a new crew arrives.

How fast does the ISS travel?

17,150 miles an hour, about 30 times faster than a Boeing 747 jet.

What happens to waste and garbage?

They seal it in bags and put it in a cargo spacecraft, which either lands on Earth or burns up in the air.

Which countries have launched astronauts with their own rockets?

The U.S., China, and Russia. Astronauts from other countries travel on U.S. or Russian rockets.

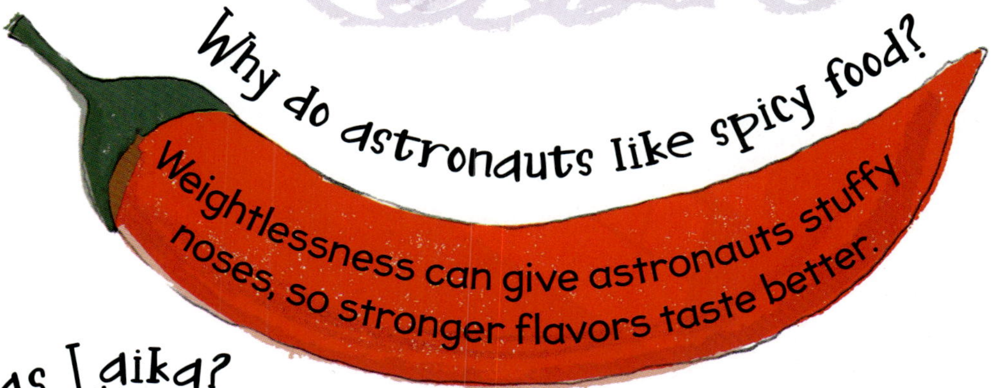

Why do astronauts like spicy food?

Weightlessness can give astronauts stuffy noses, so stronger flavors taste better.

Who was Laika?

A dog—and the first living creature to orbit Earth in 1957.

When did the first astronauts go to the ISS?

In 2000, and there have been astronauts on board ever since.

How long will footprints stay on the moon?

Millions of years because there is no air on the moon to blow them away.

Glossary

buoyancy the ability to float in water or other liquid

monitor to watch and check the progress of something

neutral in the middle, not on either side

orbit to travel around something in a curved path, or the path itself

solar having to do with the sun

tether something like a rope used to tie two things together

Index